Why can't I... Why can't I... Why can't I...
can't I... Why can't I... Why can't I... Wh...
I... Why can't I... Why can't I... Why can...
Why can't I... Why can't I... Why can't I...
can't I... Why can't I... Why can't I... Why...
I... Why can't I... Why can't I... Why can...
Why can't I... Why can't I... Why can't I...
can't I... Why can't I... Why can't I... Why...
I... Why can't I... Why can't I... Why can...
Why can't I... Why can't I... Why can't I...
can't I... Why can't I... Why can't I... Why...
I... Why can't I... Why can't I... Why can...
Why can't I... Why can't I... Why can't I

Why can't I...
eat just candy?

and other questions
about my body

Why can't I...

eat just candy?

and other questions
about my body

Ruth Thomson

Thameside Press

Distributed in the United States by
Smart Apple Media
1980 Lookout Drive
North Mankato, MN 56003

Text copyright © Ruth Thomson 2001

Editor: Claire Edwards
Designer: Jacqueline Palmer
Picture researcher: Diana Morris
Consultant: Anne Goldsworthy

Printed in Hong Kong

9 8 7 6 5 4 3 2 1

Library of Congress Cataloging-in-Publication Data

Thomson, Ruth.
    Eat just candy? : and other questions about my body / Ruth Thomson.
        p. cm. -- (Why can't I)
    Includes index.
    ISBN 1-930643-01-2
        1. Body, Human--Juvenile literature. [1. Body, Human--Miscellanea. 2. Questions and
    answers.] I. Title. II. Series.

    QM27 .T474 2001
    612--dc21

                                                        2001027183

Picture acknowledgements:
Paul Barton/Stockmarket: 25cr.
Ed Bock/Stockmarket: 25c.
Nancy Brown/Stockmarket: 24cl, 29b.
DigitalVision: 9, 13, 15r, 20t & background,
  21t & background, 26t, 30b.
Claire Paxton: 5, 12tl, 12cl, 12bl, 21br, 26b, 29c.
Tom Stewart/Stockmarket: 25cl.
Superstock: 23t.

All other photography Ray Moller.

Contents

Why can't I look like my best friend?

Because no one in the world looks quite like you.

Everyone has a head, body, legs, and arms, but some things help make people look different.

You get the color of your hair, skin and eyes from your parents. The way you look is a mixture of your relatives.

Why won't my body bend all over?

Because your bones can't bend.

There are hundreds of strong, hard bones inside your body. Your body would be floppy without them.

You can only bend your body at places where two bones meet. These places are called joints.

Why shouldn't I watch TV all day?

Because your body works best if you use it.

Walking, running, and jumping makes your bones and muscles stronger. Moving about helps your heart and lungs work better.

Why can't my heart ever have a rest?

Because if your heart stopped, so would you.

Your heart is like a pump
that never stops beating
and never gets tired.

Every time your heart beats,
it pushes blood around your body.
The blood is full of goodness
from the air you breathe
and the food you eat.

Why can't I hold my breath for very long?

Because you need to keep breathing to stay alive.

When you breathe in, you suck in air. Air has an invisible gas in it called oxygen, which your body needs.

When you breathe out, you push out stale air that your body no longer wants.

Why can't I see in the dark?

Because your eyes need light to see.

The black circles in your eyes are holes called pupils. Light comes into your eyes through your pupils.

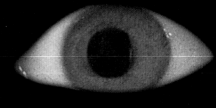

Why do I blink?

Because if you didn't,
your eyes would soon feel sore.

When you blink, your eyelids
are like windshield wipers.
They wipe tears across your eyes.
This keeps them damp and free of dirt.

Why can't I eat just candy?

Because you would soon be ill.

Food is your body's fuel.
You need a mixture of different
foods to keep your body healthy.

Milk and meat help you grow.
Bread and pasta give you
lots of energy. Fruit and
vegetables keep you well.

17

Why can't I stop smelling things?

Because your nose is made for catching smells.

Millions of tiny hairs inside your nose catch smells. When you have a cold, your nose gets blocked up, so the hairs can't catch the smells around you.

Why do I have to go to the bathroom?

Because your body needs to get rid of food and water it doesn't use.

Your body takes in nutrients from your food and drink.

You go to the bathroom to get rid of any leftovers.

Why do I shiver when I'm cold?

Because shivering is one way your body tries to warm you up.

When your body gets very cold, the muscles under your skin start twitching. Moving muscles make you feel warmer.

Why do I sweat when I'm hot?

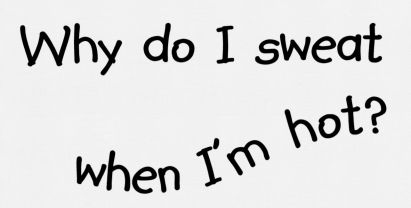

Because sweating is one way your body tries to cool you down.

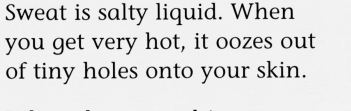

Sweat is salty liquid. When you get very hot, it oozes out of tiny holes onto your skin.

When the sweat dries, it makes your body feel cooler.

Why do I have to wash?

Because if you didn't,
you would start to smell
very bad!

Dirt sticks to your skin.
The dirt contains
tiny living things,
which can make you
smelly or even ill.

When you take
a bath or shower,
you wash them away.

Why can't I stay up all night?

Because your brain and body need a rest at the end of the day.

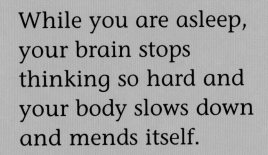

While you are asleep, your brain stops thinking so hard and your body slows down and mends itself.

Why can't I stay young forever?

Because you can't stop your body from changing.

Your body keeps growing and changing very slowly from the day you are born.

You will stop growing taller when you are about 18. But your body will never stop changing and you will never stop learning new things.

Body words

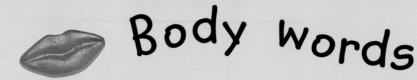

blood Blood carries important things such as oxygen and food to every part of your body.

bones The hard parts of your body. Your bones are joined together to make a framework called a skeleton.

brain The body's computer. It controls how your body works, and receives and sends messages to the rest of your body.

ear The body's microphone. It picks up sounds so that you can hear.

eye The body's camera. It lets in light so that you can see.

heart The body's pump. It sends blood all around your body.

joint The place where two bones meet. You can bend your body at the joints.

lungs The body's breathing machines. They supply your body with fresh oxygen and push out stale air.

muscles Things that move parts of your body.

All these words or phrases include a part of the body. Can you find out what they mean?

eyes
- an eye opener
- eye-catching
- to keep your eyes peeled

ears
- within earshot
- prick up your ears
- in one ear and out at the other

teeth
- by the skin of your teeth
- to have a sweet tooth

thumb
- thumbs up
- twiddle your thumbs

tongue
- to hold your tongue
- at the tip of the tongue
- tongue twister

nails
- nail-biting

breath
- out of breath
- save your breath
- hold your breath

hair
- let your hair down
- out of your hair

heart
- learn by heart
- with all my heart

hand
- to lend a hand
- handmade

arm
- at arm's length
- with open arms

nose
- nosy
- to follow your nose

brain
- brainy
- brainwave

feet
- to put your foot down
- to find your feet

Notes for parents and teachers

Read this book through so that children become familiar with the ideas in it, and with specific words about the body. Then you may like to try out these activities that reinforce some of the ideas and give the children further talking points.

This is me
Talk to children about how they would describe themselves to someone who has never met them. Discuss their distinguishing details—the color and length of their hair, the color of their eyes, their favorite clothes. Ask them to make a color picture or collage of themselves, which includes these details.

Eat up!
Look at the pictures of different foods in the book. Encourage children to think about other foods that help them grow, give them energy, or keep them healthy. Ask children to draw a picture of their favorite meal on a paper plate or on a round piece of paper.

Wiggle waggle

Ask children to invent movements to exercise different parts of their body—including some unusual parts, such as the little toe, the chin, or eyebrows, and even the ears. They may enjoy doing this to music.

After their exercise, ask children what they notice about their bodies—are they hot, sweaty, breathing faster, or tired? Can they think of any parts of the body that they didn't exercise? Can they think of any parts of the body they can't exercise (hair, nails, teeth)?

Growing all the time

Help children to compare photographs of themselves taken at different ages (especially baby photos and some taken most recently). Encourage them to talk about the differences they notice. How have their features, hair, and bodies changed?

Talk about the things children are doing in the photos, so that they become aware of their changing abilities.

Index